2.50

TECHNIQUES

OF SCULPTURE

〰〰〰

"THE AMERICAN SOLDIER"—JACOB EPSTEIN—MODERN ENGLISH—BRONZE

In this powerful head the sculptor has captured character. A vibrating surface is achieved through the skillful use of light and shadow. The feeling of spontaneity in the use of light and dark intensifies emotional content. You can almost feel the guy think.

TECHNIQUES

OF SCULPTURE

A Simple Creative Approach

By RUTH GREEN HARRIS

and GIROLAMO PICCOLI

Former head of Sculpture Division of the
New York City WPA Art Project.

Former teacher of Sculpture at the Layton
School of Art, Milwaukee, Wis.

Former teacher at the School Art League,
New York City.

Teaching at present at the Hessian Hills
School, Croton-on-Hudson, and at the
Art Workshop, New York City.

HARPER & BROTHERS PUBLISHERS

NEW YORK AND LONDON 1942

TECHNIQUES OF SCULPTURE

FIRST EDITION

A-R

CONTENTS

PREFACE

~~~~~~

AMERICAN artists today are concerned with creating works of art that will enrich and expand American life. They are no longer satisfied with acting a special part for a small and special group. Like the rest of us, they long to do a useful job for a large and interested public. All over the country you will find earnest artists discussing the material and spiritual elements of their product as all of us discuss the value of our product to a consumer, the tried and experimental materials of which it is made, the various ways of reaching our public and the creative energy that goes into a job.

But there still exists a gap between the artist and the public he longs to serve. For the usefulness of a product depends not only on the product but also on the consumer. He must be prepared to receive it. There would not be much sense putting a good engine in a car for a man who mistakes it for a horse-drawn vehicle. There is not much sense publishing books for a man who has not learned to read. There is not much sense designing great works of sculpture for those who are not equipped to feel their greatness.

vii

ACKNOWLEDGMENT

The publisher and the authors acknowledge gratefully the permission of the American sculptor, Nat Werner, for the use of his photograph on the jacket—which shows him roughing out a piece of stone as discussed in Chapter VI.

However, today in America not only the artist is trying to reach out to the public. The public also is trying to reach out to the artist, trying to learn to read the artist's message and so learn to need the artist's product.

The Federal Art Project has been partly responsible for bringing artist and public in closer accord. The public wants to know more about the painting and sculpture its taxes buy and the artist works with a sense of responsibility toward a great patron that he has not known for centuries.

This isn't only wishful conversation. By way of our experience as teacher and critic we know that the artist's ever-increasing sense of responsibility and an ever-increasing interest in the fine arts on the part of the general public date from the introduction into American life of the WPA art projects. People come to art classes; people read the art pages of their newspapers and with a growing sense of authority criticize the critic. It would seem that people even look at works of art.

Not only artists look, write letters and come to classes. A cross section of the public is displaying an impatience to know more and understand more in every medium. But there has been a natural renascence of interest in sculpture. For sculpture during its greatest periods has been a public art.

This interest introduced the authors of this book to each other. As teacher and critic we found ourselves operating along the same channel, answering the same questions and within our respective spheres giving the same answers to an eager public.

Many are bewildered. Bewilderment is often rooted in the assumption that in a creative work of art the technical and the aesthetic are two problems. This is a basic error. They are one. Technique embodies aesthetics and aesthetics embodies technique. The sort of statement people make and the kind of question they ask have brought us to the conclusion that much of the confusion of mind lies in the mistaken belief that an artist turns off his aesthetic, creative heart and mind when he exercises his technical hand. And so we decided to write a technical book on sculpture from an aesthetic springboard. To our knowledge, no such book has been written.

It is simple, designed primarily for the amateur and for the beginner. It is sound. We believe it can be valuable to the most serious artist.

It is purposefully short. We have tried to present basic principles freed of cluttering detail and, so far as it is humanly possible, of personal prejudice. Using basic principles of procedure only to forestall basic error, we hope the student will follow his natural bent and develop his natural talent.

The more you practice the art of sculpture the more you realize the close interlocking of the aesthetic with the technical. This realization will help you bridge the gap between yourself and works of art, if such gap exists, and will prepare you to receive the artist's message, the idea within his work. Good works of art will become as needful and as useful as good books, good music, and good everything.

This does not mean that a profound philosophy is locked in every piece of carved stone. We are not always in a mood for profound ideas. We need also the gaiety, wit and humor that sculpture no less than books, music, and the movies can provide.

We should like to make a few suggestions on the way to use this book. You will notice that we have said (hoping you will forgive the peremptory tone in our voices), "Read this chapter through before starting work. Reread it after you have started work." Now we urge you to read the whole book through before you start the first problem, omitting only the chapter on waste molds because that is a purely mechanical process for reproducing a work, not creating it.

We believe that reading the book as a whole will give you a general notion of what we are endeavoring to explain. Technique and aesthetics are inseparable. Reading the book will give you a kind of "feel" for sculpture. Then after you have started on one problem, on modeling a small figure or on carving in stone, you might read the whole book again. For as soon as you have taken tools and materials in hand you will bring to the whole subject that indispensable feel for it that will make every move more reasonable and in a large way relate the whole subject. For whether you are carving or modeling, first principles are the same. But a practical interpretation of principles depends on development. This subject is like every other. The more you bring to it the more you take from it. That is why we suggest rereading. Certain statements which at first may seem obscure will become inevitably clear.

Please bear with us while we make one more suggestion. No matter in what medium you may be working, we recommend that you reread the chapter on design, for we believe this will ultimately serve as a timesaver; will help keep you from floundering in technical bewilderment.

We have included a paragraph on enlarging. This does not involve you as a student. We have touched upon it because it is a sculptor's problem, one that someday you may feel inclined to pursue.

That part of the text which refers specifically to the photographs will stress some particular point that the reproduction illustrates: compact design, design in relation to material, balance, or movement. Each reproduction will illustrate not one but many points. Try training yourself to look for others. The greater your experience, of course, the more you will find to enjoy.

But if examination of sculpture is limited to the reproductions in this book then it has dismally failed in its purpose.

We hope that, alive and receptive, you will stop to explore with heart and mind every piece of sculpture you can get your eyes on. Gradually you will find yourself equipped to be critical of what has failed; and equipped to enjoy with all that's in you what is fine in the sculpture of all times and all periods: Cambodian,

African, Etruscan, Egyptian, Aztec, Roman, Romanesque, early Greek—everything.

And above all try to receive wholeheartedly the work of your contemporary American colleagues. For, as you have seen, they are longing to serve you.

TECHNIQUES

OF SCULPTURE

Chapter 1. DESIGN

〰〰〰〰〰〰〰〰〰〰〰〰〰〰〰〰〰

THIS is a discussion of design. Read it through once. It may make hard reading now, but we feel sure that as soon as the clay or the stone is on your model stand the various suggestions we make will begin to explain themselves. In the following chapters you will find step-by-step directions. Even though the various laws of design will be repeated as the need for each arises, we suggest that you reread this chapter during the progress of your work.

Sculpture has three dimensions—length, breadth and thickness. When we look about us, when we make pictures in our minds, the things we see and the pictures we see with our mind's eye are not flat but three-dimensional. Therefore, working in sculpture is one of the most natural ways of working, because the artist need not transform his ideas and round them out on a flat surface, on paper or canvas. Of all the mediums, of all the materials with which an artist works, sculptural mediums, either modeled or carved, make forms which come closest to the forms we create in imagination.

Children love to model castles and cities and people in mud and snow and sand. Some grownups call these modeled pictures mud pies and hardly bother looking at them. And yet they often actually burst with enchantment dear to human imagination. Somehow the adult may fail to get this quality into his work. Why? Because he is troubled by technical problems. Don't be repressed by technique. Don't *worry* about technique.

For anyone can learn it. The important thing is to try to recapture the confidence and freedom of a child. Your work will be on a higher plane because you bring to it greater wisdom and richer experience. The sculptor, tapping his wisdom and experience, puts into solid form the things he sees clearly in imagination and feels strongly about. Educators call this natural process liberating the creative impulse.

In order to learn technical processes it is necessary to practice technical processes. But as you work you will feel skill becoming a part of yourself. You will feel it becoming a good tool and not a hindrance to the natural creative process. You will feel yourself mastering your craft and making it serve your needs. It is a glorious sensation.

You've decided to start work. Maybe you want to make a statement about a great friend. He has something you've always been crazy about—determination or courage or generosity or humor. Though he is in the next room or the next town you can see him in imagina-

"HAWK GOD HORUS"—EGYPTIAN—XXX DYNASTY—BASALT

Here dignity of design embodies the nature of the material, hard basalt.
It lends itself to no deep undercuts or fussy details. Though this figure is
only about 30″ high, the proportions of the design suggest a monument of
heroic size.

"PIETA"—MICHELANGELO—STONE CARVING—UNFINISHED

In this composition by Michelangelo the form and the design express intensely the conception of the artist. By way of design, each figure expresses emotional quality. There is a deliberate change in the scale of the various figures. Yet the group with thrust, counter-thrust and transition is built up to form a magnificent unified whole.

tion. Any quality and your feeling about that quality can be put into sculpture.

Some knowledge of the material you're working in will help clarify the statement you wish to make, because it will help you shape and design the material.

Let's use a homely example. The cut of a woolen suit can be made just as becoming as the cut of a chiffon dress. But the nature of the material, thick or flimsy, will suggest the cut. What you want to say about your friend can be modeled in clay or cut in stone, but for each process you would design differently, just as you would go about designing a dress of one material differently from the dress of another, though both must be becoming to the same person.

Put this in a sculptor's language. The artist works within the limitations of his material.

This isn't as complex as it sounds. Say "wood" to yourself; then "stone." Different shapes come to mind. It is bad taste to try to make wood do something that is natural to stone.

You are working in what is called a plastic material. You are not working in flesh or lace. You want your work to look like sculpture and not like flesh or lace.

Roughly, we work in two mediums: a hard, permanent material that is cut directly like wood or stone and an impermanent material like clay or plasteline. From the clay model a cast is made in some permanent material like bronze. A sculptor seldom makes his own bronze. He makes the plaster from which the bronze is cast.

3

Stone (marble, of course, is a stone) is massive and heavy. The design must be well supported at the base and avoid extended parts, a kicked-out leg, for example. Because the surface is hard, stone carving should not become too intricate or fussy. Michelangelo is supposed to have said, "A marble statue should be so created that it can be rolled down from the mountain tops without mutilation. Anything that breaks off is superfluous." Working within the limitations of this material suggests large, simple forms.

You will find that you will even want to work within the limitations of a particular piece of stone. Say you have an idea and some marble. It is standing comfortably. You place it in a horizontal position. It looks less comfortable. You move it this way and that. It feels best, most natural, in the position in which you instinctively placed it when you brought it into the workshop. Of course you can chip away and make your stone stand in any position; but if you do so, will you ever completely enjoy the finished work? Won't there always be a hangover memory of the comfort of that stone as you first saw it? You need not discard your idea. You can, instead, restudy it, look for another piece of stone, or work your idea in a different medium, in clay, perhaps, with plans for casting.

Practically anything can be modeled in clay though your design will depend on the material in which you plan to cast it. The flexibility of clay is its greatest shortcoming and its greatest asset. It is a shortcoming because the very tractableness of the material sometimes leads

"Figure"—Girolamo Piccoli—Modern
American

In this figure the long rhythmic planes of
limbs and drapery pass from one form to
another with quiet and balanced movement.

"Maine Cat"—William Zorach—Modern American—Granite

In this composition the artist has used naturalistic shapes without sacrifice to plastic realism. The assembled elements form a compact design.

sculptors to forget large sculptural values. It is an asset because clay seems willing to concede to the subtlest ideas.

Not only different materials but different ideas suggest different distributions of weight. If you have in your mind an idea about joy your very body seems to respond to the word and the weight of your body seems to lift. You may raise your arms. If you have in your mind an idea about sleep, muscles relax and the weight falls. But no matter what your conception, weight must be distributed so that the subject supports itself. And though, in the spirit of joy, your sculpture may raise its arms, the weight of the rest of the figure must be ready to carry raised arms in whatever material you are using. Different mediums will solve the problem in different ways.

Assume that you have chosen an idea to be executed in stone. Is the design suitable to stone? Maybe the figure stands on one foot. Though it might collapse in the process it is possible to carve this figure. But you would be violating the inner nature of the material. Neither you nor your public will ever thoroughly enjoy the finished work.

Once you have started work you will be able to feel in your very bones the difference between the sense of the completed movement you want to achieve in sculpture and a sense of what artists call arrested action. You will not be pleased with a work that looks as though it had never finished and would never finish what it is about to do. Such sculpture will forever create in your

body and in your mind a dis-ease, a discomfort. This is
another of those natural laws of sculptural form that
is difficult to grasp as you read the words but will be
even more difficult to avoid as you develop your piece.
The kind of sculptor who has made technique an end in
itself instead of a good tool is often in danger of leaving
the action incomplete.

Don't work from photographs. They will hurt your
work in many ways. The camera's one eye gives only
the illusion of depth. Shape is obscured by light and
shade. Too often the camera catches arrested motion.
In sculpture motion flows, one form to another.

The artist in you will design your sculpture. Design
in sculpture is the harmonious and moving organization
of planes and masses. The organization of small forms
is based on the large masses. If you organize the sub-
divisions without first realizing the big forms you lose
all feeling of sculpture.

As we have said, sculpture is a three-dimensional art.
You are working in solids. But not at any point in your
sculpture as you turn it must it look as though limited
to only one face. Every part, every plane must flow
into every other so that the eye travels with the flow no
matter from what angle you see the work. To do this,
try to think of your design as a possible spiral. This,
too, sounds difficult. But once you start working you
will find it easier to make the planes flow around than
to make a series of unrelated surfaces.

In two senses, sculptural forms must be conceived
from within: from within the heart and mind and from

6

"Workers"—Milton Hebald—Modern American

In a work composed of many parts the movement and flow of the design
create a unified whole.

GARDEN FIGURE DESIGNED FOR BRONZE BY GIROLAMO PICCOLI

Here you see the ability of bronze to support an extended mass. Due to the nature of the material the extended weight is properly and comfortably carried.

within the piece itself. This is another way of preventing work from looking like a series of unrelated surfaces or as though made of bits stuck on. Think of forms radiating from an imaginary core. Pretend for a moment that your sculpture is transparent. Imagine that you can see every form going back, flowing back to a central core and being pushed out from within, again in spiral fashion, around the core.

Open spaces or "negative forms" are part of the design. If a figure, for example, stands with one hand on hip, the space between the body and the crooked elbow is not just a hollow but a shape, part of the design and as important as every other part.

Don't be too worried about proportions. Don't worry if a jowl becomes heavy or an arm long or an ankle thick. Artistically speaking, proportion means that the size of one area looks well with the size of another and that this relationship is appropriate to the material and the idea. You may find that something about a long arm, a thick ankle, or a heavy jowl helps express what you have in mind about an idea or a person.

From the beginning artists have worked for expression. Design must have expression. But expression is not only facial, as you very well know. Without seeing his face but only his back, you can tell by the way a man walks whether he is tired or full of energy. Design will vary with what you want to say—agitation may create many violent planes; peace, a few smooth planes.

Design is composed of many elements. Assume that the big emotional forms so well established in your mind have taken shape. Then comes a refining of those forms in a manner that will not fuddle but will strengthen the idea. The contributing elements in design are called repeat, contrast, texture and color.

Take as an example a good piece of jazz, not because it is an exact example but a familiar one. Most of us hear jazz on the radio; many of us dance to it. And, by the way, we have come to discriminating conclusions about its quality. Assume that the tune is the big idea. Contributing to that idea, there may be the repeated note of a drum; the contrast of high and low notes; there is texture, achieved by the different sound quality of different instruments, a saxophone against a clarinet; and there is color, a variation in loudness and softness.

Carry this over into sculpture. Certain forms will be repeated, a triangular plane, perhaps. Rounder forms may contrast the triangle. A smooth area against a rougher one makes texture and light and shade, the movement in and out gives color.

This sounds more complex than it is, for your sculpture as it grows cannot escape these elements. But you will be more interested in your work if you recognize them, deal with them consciously, and control them. We will suggest, when that time comes, that in the beginning you start with not too complex an idea. We will suggest one simple statement about something or somebody you know well. Don't worry about the technique of these contributory elements.

At least one glorious surprise is due the beginner. You will find that you know far more about the human figure than you had any idea of—which is natural enough. It belongs, after all, to your own species. Before starting work get into the position that the figure in your imagination must take in order wholeheartedly to express your idea and emotion. Close your eyes. You become aware of the stresses and pulls that this idea demands of your body. Try to visualize the body in this position and draw on the vision that has been created in your mind.

We hope you have not become impatient with this discussion on design, because we feel that it will give you a kind of definition of your medium. And though each phase will be repeated with special reference to your work in progress we would like you to reread this chapter after you have finished modeling your first subject.

Chapter II. MODELING A SMALL FIGURE

~~~~~~

YOU are now starting a design. You are building it up without the aid of an armature, without the interior framework that must be used to support any large quantity of clay. This model therefore will be small.

We suggest it be small enough to fit into a cracker or a sugar tin about 10 by 8 inches. Filling the cover with clay gives a platform on which to model. By fitting the can well into the cover, you devise a reasonably airtight compartment. Work in progress must be kept moist. An airtight compartment keeps the clay in condition.

Some beginners may wish to use plasteline. It need not be kept moist. However, we do not recommend it. For clay is more *plastic*, more pliable, more willingly worked. A small clay design similar to the one you first execute, will harden and can be preserved, for no foreign substance like an armature is introduced. Plasteline sculpture does not harden and has therefore no endurance. It is relatively expensive.

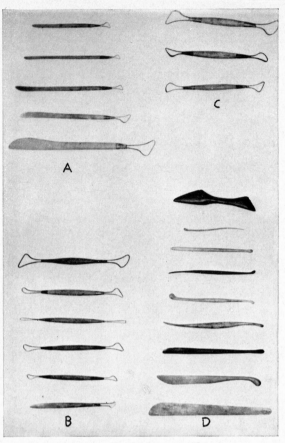

Types of Clay Modeling Tools

Hands are the best tools. Collect your tools slowly learning through experience those most useful to your own purpose. The first purchase might be a spatula with a wire end—medium size.

(A) Spatulas with wire ends.

(B) Wire end tools of various shapes and sizes, useful for gouging out depressions in the design.

(C) Tools with ends of twisted wire useful for roughing out; cutting away large amounts of clay; achieving texture.

(D) Spatula and knob and tools. The spatula end is used for shaping, establishing planes, cutting away surface clay (the spatula is a delicate tool and should not be used for gouging). Knob ends are used for shaping surface hollows too small for fingers to reach—ears, nostrils and other small undercuts in the design.

We suggest keeping the clay in a large garbage can. Clay should be sufficiently moist to work easily and yet not so sticky that it clings to the hands. Students often start working clay too wet. Clay that sticks to the fingers lessens their efficiency. They become less sensitive tools, with a tendency to blur the surface. No hands are at their best with gloves on. If you have made your clay too wet, knead out the water on a dry board; if too dry, add a little water. Make a ball of clay. If none sticks to the hands you have achieved the proper consistency, the consistency of putty, not glue.

You are now ready to make a small piece of sculpture. We ask you to work from memory without a model, using one of the many conceptions we hope came to mind when you read the first chapter. We suggest the simplest. A *compact* design, one that hugs itself, one without extended parts.

Try in your mind's eye to imagine it finished. You know what you want it to say. Is it sculpturesque? Although your sense of sculpture will grow as you work, try to answer this question in the light of the discussion on design.

It is most important to work on a level with the eye. Students have a tendency to place their work at an uncomfortable height. If you have no model stand, cut down a bathroom stool to the proper height when placed on a table.

Now fill the cover of your can with clay until the clay is level with the edge of the cover. Place this, as we have said, at eye level. If you work too high or too low the forms become distorted.

Think of your conception. Examine it mentally for big forms so intently that the details melt into them. Build this up quickly on the clay you have put into the cover of the can. Just take lumps of clay into your hand and put them where you need them, giving them shape immediately. Shape with your tools and with your hands. Keep design forever in mind: the spiral around the central core; the spiraling surface with one form flowing into another.

Don't complete one part at a time but keep the whole work at the same stage as you go along. Don't try to model the folds of a dress, for example, before the main action is indicated in a large way. Many students start by completing each part. This hampers those changes you feel are necessary to the development of the big idea. Perhaps the arm should be longer. You are reluctant to lengthen the arm because you have spent so much time modeling its details and don't want to destroy what seems finished. The work at all stages must be at the same stage of progression.

You will find as you work that one form influences another. This is true of your own body. If you lift one shoulder (lift it now) the direction of your body naturally follows that movement.

The torso of the human figure can be divided into two main forms. The thorax, the part of the body between the neck and the abdomen, and the pelvis—the bony girdle that joins the legs to the body (hips). Movement proceeds from the torso, and the most expressive, wholehearted movements (as dancers know) take place between these two main forms. These two sections are connected by a section of the spinal column called the lumbar region. When thinking of the torso imagine the action an arrangement of these two main forms in relation to one another. Then the action throughout will fall in place. Don't concentrate too much on these scientific facts or burden yourself with them. We throw them in as useful suggestions, for the work will be stronger if action grows from some given point. Don't let the suggestion interfere with your design, which can, as a matter of fact, make its own laws.

Action is not necessarily violent action. There is action in repose. In art, action may be defined as distribution of weight. If anything is out of balance it is likely to have too much weight, too much force, too much action in one part in relation to another.

We are throwing in some hints now about approximate relative sizes in the human figure. This approximate scale may be useful to you if you feel stuck. Hands, for example. To get a notion of their size, place your hand against your face and look into the mirror. Beginners are likely to make hands and feet too small. Small hands and feet weaken the conception.

A figure is from seven and one-half to eight heads high. From the top of the head to the crotch equals half the figure. From the chin to the nipples of the breast measures one head length. From nipples to navel one head. From navel to crotch another. The length of a foot equals one-half the distance from the knee to the floor.

You have completed the first stage and are satisfied with the action, the balance and the big forms. It is a good plan now to move the work about. Just lift up the cover of the can in which you have been modeling and place it on the mantelpiece and then on the floor. Are you still satisfied? Is the design just as comfortable in these positions and in this new light as it was at eye level?

Perhaps you and a friend are working together. You will find that your works are unlike. Your handwriting is unlike that of your friends. These differences in personality heighten the character of your work.

Let us assume that at this point you have finished work for the day. Take your can and fit the upper edge right down into the cover in which you have been working, pressing it firmly. This will keep the work in as airtight a condition as possible and prevent it from drying.

If you find, however, that when you next go to work the clay has become too dry, you can easily bring it back to a workable condition. Make holes with a nail and fill them with water. Place a wet cloth over the clay. In a model as small as this one, it will become wet enough to work in a few hours. If you are prevented from working for two or three days look at your clay to be assured it has not dried so much that you will be unable to work it when working time comes.

Plasteline, of course, need not be wetted.

If you find that your work has moved or shifted, take an orange stick and shove it down through the top. To

Courtesy of the New York City WPA Art Project
"FIGURE"—JOSEPH KONZAL—MODERN AMERICAN

With apposing forms, thrusting the movement of one form against the
movement of another, this artist has composed a compact design.

A III Century Greek terra cotta designed to be executed in clay
without the support of an armature.

preserve this piece, remove the orange stick when finished. If you do not remove it, the dry clay will crumble away from the stick, from any inserted foreign body.

When modeling smaller forms, draperies, clothes, details in hands and feet and face and hair develop the design elements: color, texture, and repeat. You have probably visualized your idea clothed. Clothes are natural to us. Our kind of clothes. Some ham sculptors have a notion that only Greek togas make good sculpture. Anything can make good sculpture.

You'll find now that the smaller tools come in handy.

You want to simplify details; don't get them overworked and fussy. A fold in the clothes can stress the direction of a plane and emphasize the emotional quality of the work. Perhaps a shoulder is raised, indicating pride. The line of the drapery can help make the gesture more decisive. Don't forget the spiral within the small parts reaching out toward the larger ones.

By way of the various elements of design, details give enriching opportunity. Though in a single work all the design elements may be used, one will dominate. Feel that you are emphasizing the element most necessary to the strengthening of your idea.

No one element should be done to death. Repetitions, for example, become monotonous if they are not opposed by other elements, contrast of large and small forms, relation of curves to angles, harmonious radiation from the central core. Others will present themselves as you work.

15

Though you consider these elements you must never let them replace your main idea. Idealess design is mere decoration.

Avoid cutting into the big forms you have established. This is a student's tendency. You have established the big plane of an arm area, for example. Don't let folds of drapery cut into the arm itself, for the arm plus its drapery have determined the volume of this area.

You have finished your first piece of sculpture. If you have worked in clay it will harden and can be preserved—an example of your first work. (If one has been inserted, don't fail to remove the orange stick.) Done in either plasteline or clay, this can serve as a model for a larger work. It can be cast in another material. This compact design is also suitable for cutting in stone. The next work will be a head on a larger scale. But for this you will need an armature.

Chapter III. MODELING A PORTRAIT BUST IN CLAY

~~~~~~

THE urge to make portraits is strong in the human race.

In a fine portrait not only the flesh and bone but the heart and mind are presented.

You have often heard the phrase "ideal portrait." It is the likeness of an artist's vision and no less real for describing in whatever material the sculptor may use the appearance of an inner vision rather than the appearance of an actual man.

We imagine, for example, that we know what Moses looked like. When we think of him certain shapes and characteristics come to mind, a certain grandeur and nobility, a certain interlocking of compassion with anger. We know very well that no contemporary portrait of Moses exists. The established portrait is the likeness of an artist's vision. The one we see today and almost take for granted was Michelangelo's. His portrait established the characterful form. Other artists consulted the famous monument, the Moses we know so well, almost as though they were reading character not from sculpture but from life itself.

Supposing Michelangelo had not created the Mosaic type, we are equipped to call on our own inner visions and create our own portraits. We can still do so. Ours are no less "real" than the great Italian master's.

Primitive man often made portraits of his gods. Sometimes they were in the form of masks designed to be worn on ceremonial occasions. Thus man ennobled his own stature. Though made to quicken the devotion of simpler people, ancient god-portraits touch our emotions today. For fundamental structure does not change any more than fundamental behavior changes. Man still weeps and laughs.

Whether creating a god or executing a portrait commission an artist still uses imagination rooted in the experience he has gained by observing the human countenance in moments of anger, exaltation, love, heroism, horror.

Sculptors have made portraits of gods and kings and friends and relations and patrons and heroes and statesmen. No matter from what source it derives, pauper or prince, the less an artist calls on his imagination and experience and the more he imitates feature for feature, the less vigorous the art becomes.

The forms in a carved or modeled head are modified by the culture and tradition of the period in which the artist is working, the materials he uses, and the use to which the work is to be put. A Pharaoh's portrait in

Courtesy of the Metropolitan Museum of Art, New York

HEAD FROM A BUST OF QUEEN NEFERTITI—PLASTER CAST FROM PAINTED
LIMESTONE

A beautiful example of head, neck and shoulders in relation to each other.
Note with what strength and grace the neck flows from the shoulders.

granite for an Egyptian tomb is differently designed from a head in bronze by Epstein for the table of a twentieth century English drawing room.

In the tradition of our own day, many artists make portraits that are recognizable likenesses and vigorously artistic at the same time. The artist uses his imagination, experience, knowledge of design, and the materials he is working in. And with a sense of the tradition and culture of our time he does not imitate the art of Greece or Rome.

Before you begin we shall make a couple of suggestions. Don't try to do the portrait of a hairy face, because it is difficult to reach the determinating and characterful shapes under a lot of beard. However, this is probably an academic warning, for beards and mustachios have gone out of fashion.

And do not start with the portrait of a child, for two reasons. First, and most important, when a head is still in the process of developing, character is so subtle that it takes more than a beginner's experience to discover it. Then, too, it is hard to get a child to sit long enough even if we do not demand any fixedness of face or body. But at least it helps not to have the subject crawling on the floor or running in and out of the room.

We also advise that you choose for your first subject someone you know well; someone whose character you have learned by heart.

For the first work, we suggest that you include the shoulders.

Character in a head follows the general design of

character in a body. You know from your own experience the shape of laughter or sadness in a mouth. You have already learned from experience gained in modeling a small figure the emotional quality of upmoving planes. We have seen expressions derived from the direction a shape takes under certain circumstances enter our very language. We talk of feeling down in the mouth, of feeling uplifted.

If your sitter is not well known to you, first and foremost study character. By way of your experience with character you know almost subconsciously that certain characteristics take certain shapes. By their faces you have often judged the character of strangers in a crowd. The fellow standing next to you has a mean or a noble look. Differentiating shapes is what the primitive understood so well. It is impossible for us to tell you in any accurate way the shape of a certain quality. This you learn from experience alone.

As you work around the head, watching it from every aspect, you see every part of the design related to every other one. You avoid dull and jumpy areas or the look of things stuck on. You remember the never-ending flow of a design and the contributing elements: repeat, contrast, texture, and color.

We repeat even at the risk of boring you. (If you are bored, you will realize graphically the danger of misusing this element in your own design.) You are working in a three-dimensional medium. You are not thinking of areas with outlines. For, as you examine the model from every side, outlines are so infinitely numerous that they seem hardly to exist, as, in a way, an isolated second hardly exists, moving, as it does, so quickly to the next. If you think of your model as a series of outlines instead of forms developing from an inner core, your work will lack "plastic" value, will lack a sense of weight, the sense of a volume that can fill your hands. It will become, on the other hand, a series of cutting edges. This we stress because students who have understood the designing of a figure tend to overlook design when they face a head.

Thinking and working in outline instead of in volume and planes is against nature, for that is not the way we see things; and against the nature of a head, for it assumes a certain shape because of things happening within: structural things like bone, emotional things like anger.

We are faced with two problems. We want to make a good likeness and we want to make good sculpture. In almost every head the solving of one problem will help you solve the other. If you capture the characteristic big forms, you probably cannot avoid making the head sculpturesque. And if you make the head sculpturesque, using the big forms you discover in the head of your model, you probably cannot avoid likeness. Sometimes you hear it said that a portrait is more like the person than the person himself. This is because all unsculpturesque and uncharacterful trivialities have been omitted. Care must be taken not to create a caricature, which, as you know, is the extreme exaggeration of one part to the disadvantage of another.

Likeness cannot be caught by copying a head, feature for feature. Not only beginners fail to achieve likeness by working under the delusion that heads are made of features alone. The egglike shape of the head reveals two-thirds of the likeness. Were you to model each feature perfectly, you would still find likeness eluding you unless you had designed the features in relation to each other within the egg shape of the head. Close your eyes and think of someone you know well. Is it individual features you see with your mind's eye? All of us recognize our friends, but not by their features. All of us have seen something called "family likeness" among brothers and sisters and parents who can boast of the most varied assortment of different shaped features. Many an artist has succeeded in achieving a recognizable likeness by modeling the head oval without indicating any individual feature.

Remember how self-conscious you felt when you last had your picture taken, and how much you yourself disliked the dis-ease you saw in the print, an unnatural smirk or a taut shoulder? Therefore, try to put your sitter at ease; talk to him, maybe about the mechanics of your own work, as you start building the armature you will need for his bust. Then, sly as anything, watch what he does with his head, how he moves, and the shape of the planes on his face.

Once a person is at ease, he reveals rather than hides his character.

If you can learn to work from an easily posing model, one on whom you are not forcing immobility,

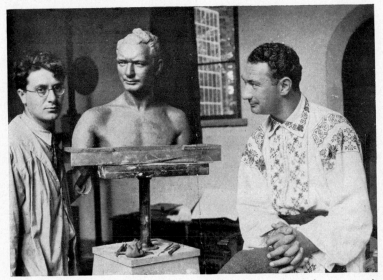

The author of *This Believing World*, Lewis Browne, posed for a portrait
bust by Girolamo Piccoli.

your victim will have a pleasanter time of it, and will co-operate more willingly. And you yourself will avoid a stiff and rigid sculpture.

From time to time, of course, you will be obliged to ask your sitter to hold the pose. But it is important to get into the habit of working from a relaxed and comfortable model. Try to do so right from the beginning.

BUST PEG

This bust will need a support called a bust peg. Take a board 16 to 18 inches square. Reinforce with cleats against the grain to prevent warping. You will need a length of wood approximately 14 inches long by 2 inches square, some lead tubing ¾ inch thick, long enough to be bent into two circular forms 6 inches in diameter, plus 4 inches for nailing. Your plumber can supply the lead. For the shoulders you will need a length of wood 12 to 14 inches long by 1 inch by 2 inches.

Nail the 1 by 2 by 14-inch length of wood to the center of your reinforced flat piece. Use pieces of wood around the base for reinforcement.

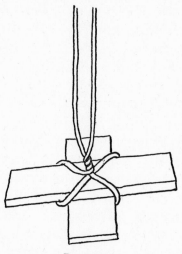

BUTTERFLY

Butterflies are hung from the armature to help support large masses of clay in the bulky portions of your design. As indicated in the drawing a cross is made by wiring together two small pieces of wood.

Shape the lead with your hands so as to form intersecting circles. Nail the ends to the upright piece and in the center place a butterfly. Nail the shoulder piece to the back of the upright sufficiently low to allow for the modeling of the neck.

We suggest that you prepare the peg for your bust

while the sitter is in the shop. While putting it together you are talking to him or persuading him to talk. Without his realizing it you are studying him. You have determined the pose. Place the sitter so that his eyes are on the level with your own. Your work, as you already know, should be at a corresponding height.

One way of avoiding the outline error is to examine the planes of the head, not only from a left-to-right direction, but from an up-and-down direction as well, looking down at both models, clay and flesh, from above and up at them from below.

The clay, about 150 pounds, should be of the same consistency as the previous clay used—pliable but not sticky.

You start by laying in the great masses, not carrying one part farther than the next. (But this, of course, you know from your experience in modeling a small figure.)

The head is an oval composed of two main masses. One is the cranium including the forehead and the upper jaw. The other is the lower jaw. It is most important to establish the relative proportion of these two areas.

Now notice the way the neck grows out of the shoulders and the placement of the head on the neck. You will find the pit of the neck at the lowest point. You will find it helpful to indicate this point at the beginning. The neck is not perpendicular but moves at a slight angle, as you can see in the reproduction of Queen Nefertiti. Note the way the Egyptian artist called on his imagination and observation for designing one of the most beautiful portraits in aesthetic history. His imagination informed him what he wanted to achieve. Through observation he learned what to stress in order to formulate his conception.

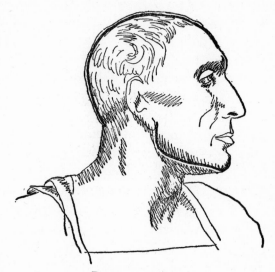

DIAGRAM OF HEAD
Drawing from Donatello showing the relation of cranium to lower jawbone.

After you have built up the main masses, the cranium and lower jaw, the neck and shoulders, draw a line through the middle of the face to establish the angle of the head. Draw a line across the eyebrows. Now set the position of the eyes. The eyes are in the middle of the oval.

The following points are given as a sort of crutch. They are those of a so-called "ideal" head, which is just

26

as much an imaginary head as one in which the design departs from the proportions. However, they are useful to know because they represent the norm, the textbook-in-anatomy head. The distance from a point between the eyebrows to the bottom of the chin equals the distance from the tip of the nose to the tragus (the little flat place in front of the opening) of the ear, which equals the distance, along the diameter, from tragus to tragus. Insert match sticks at these points when you have established them. Let the match stick protrude about ⅛ inch.

A line drawn from the eyebrows paralleling a line drawn from the bottom of the nose gives the size of

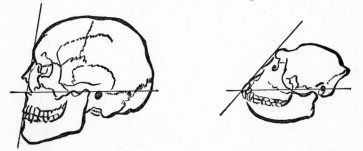

Drawing of the facial angle of a human head and the head of a monkey. The angle is greater in the human head and decreases in the lower forms of life.

the ear. In older people ears are slightly larger in proportion. They seem to grow with age. Age changes shapes. Great age in sculpture is presented, not so much by a wrinkled surface as by *form*. The "nutcracker" face is an example of changes age has wrought on structure.

27

The distance from the tragus to the back of the head is relatively less than from the tragus to the tip of the nose. This is an important proportion. The facial angle is established by an imaginary line running from the base of the nose to the tragus in relation to another line running from the base of the nose to the center of the forehead. In human beings this angle is greater than in animals. The Greeks exaggerated this angle in order to give their sculpture a noble, a divine appearance.

Every proportion will be varied by the nature of the sitter and the nature of the design. But don't rationalize. Every proportion *will* vary with the nature of the sitter, and the nature of the design. But don't fool yourself. Never seem to be satisfied with forms that have not met your primary idea by pretending that an indifferent arrangement was the way you originally meant them to go.

Besides the great masses already mentioned, the other principal masses are the forehead, cheekbones, and the structure of the nose. Model them now. Note how the cheekbones join the bridge of the nose. If you have properly distributed the masses and have studied the relative sizes and shapes, likeness should be beginning to gleam through the clay. For these masses present the most obvious differences in faces.

The upper jawbone is cylindrical in shape; the lower jawbone is as an inverted horseshoe. Study these masses (as we hope you have studied all masses) by looking up at them from underneath and down onto them from above. The mouth takes on a curved form when viewed from underneath—the corners of the mouth are the two ends of a bow.

Eyes should be studied with care. You have, of course, established their size and position, having estab-

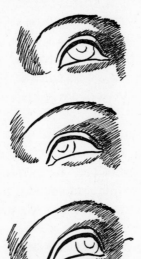

DRAWING OF EYES IN DIFFERENT POSITIONS

The shape of the areas around the eyeball is affected by the position of the eye. The raised cornea forms a bulge. The bulge alters the shape of the area it pushes out. To model the direction of eyes consider the shape of the outer area rather than the position of the pupil and iris. Cover the iris in the drawing with your finger. You still know in what direction the eye is focused.

lished the size and position of surrounding areas. You don't want to overemphasize them in sculpture and yet in life they are the feature you are most likely to look at when you are talking to a person. They are often the most expressive feature in the face and have been called

the mirrors of personality. Always remember you are
modeling clay, not human stuff, so eyes must be sym-
bolically presented. Don't overmodel them. Don't make
them fussy. The eye is a round ball. The cornea is a
crystallike form; and because it is raised from the eyeball it causes a bulge. The position of the bulge estab-
lishes the direction in which the eyes are looking.

The head is modeled. The masses have been expressed
by planes. Planes are the surfaces that bound the masses.
They are the elements of your design. Are you pleased
with the design? Now you realize that many designs
can be made from a head without sacrifice of likeness.
You have chosen to emphasize one plane, and one quality. Another sculptor may choose another.

Hair presents a glorious opportunity for design. Its
texture can be made to contrast the texture of the face.
The more or less arbitrary arrangement can be used
to balance or repeat an area. The texture can be made
to approximate the lightness or darkness of your sitter's
hair. Long smoothnesses which catch the light suggest
light hair. A relatively broken surface to which a lot of
shadow clings suggests dark hair.

Another hint, one you may have already taken uncon-
sciously, now that you are learning to know more of the
essence of your material. You do not copy the depth
of the cavities of nose and ears. This would create great
dark cavities in your sculpture that you do not see in
a flesh-and-bone head, for flesh is relatively transparent.
Clay is dense. So with a much shallower indentation
you will achieve the proper amount of shadow or color.

In giving you a lesson about the building up of a portrait head, it has been necessary (because of the nature of the medium we are using, the written word) to follow a feature-by-feature program. You have already learned not to follow this kind of program but to keep the whole head working, not carrying one part farther than another, not thinking of separate bits but of the whole design.

Before putting your work away until our next session read the chapter on keeping the clay wet.

Chapter IV. ON KEEPING THE CLAY MOIST

~~~~~~

CLAY must be kept moist. Dry clay cannot be modeled. Obviously, then, it is of greatest importance to keep it in a workable condition. You can spend hours of good time and waste hours of your model's time waiting for dry clay to recover a moist and proper state. Certainly it can be restored, but sometimes days pass before you bring back the required plasticity. If you are to be away for several days, take extra precautions. We have another suggestion to offer out of our own bitter experience. Take the precautions yourself. Don't depend on the promises of even your best friend to wet the clay during your absence. Even the most sympathetic outsider rarely respects a work during the formative state. Carelessly handled or inadequately protected, the sculpture can be ruined.

You do understand then that when you leave your work untouched for several days the precautions must be more thorough than even on those days you do not actually work.

If the clay dries too much, you are faced with complete catastrophe. It will crack, shrink away from the support, crumble and collapse.

WIRE LOOPS IN POSITION

The loops protect the delicate modeling from the heavy wet covers placed over the clay to keep it moist between working hours. The loops need only be used during the last stages.

Keep the work away from open windows and hot radiators.

The first principle is simple enough. This you learned while you were working on your small model. You remember that you fitted the can tightly down onto the cover? You made an airtight compartment. The same principle holds. Air is enemy number one. No matter what moistening methods you adopt, devising an airtight compartment is the basis of them all.

In the early stages of a bust cover the work with damp cloths and damp newspapers. Newspapers are excellent insulators. Then fit over the damp cloths some air-resisting material, rubber sheeting or oilcloth. If oilcloth is used, the oil-treated side must be put next to the cloths and newspapers, otherwise the material will disintegrate.

As work progresses you will be obliged to protect the surface modeling with the greatest care. Heavy rags rub the surface. You might adopt this method: Take a wire loop and fit the ends into the ears of the bust. Take a second loop and bisecting the first fit it into the back of the head and under the chin. Allow the loops to pass about one inch above the clay, one inch away from the work. While modeling, of course, they are removed. If you leave for several days, a few thicknesses of wet newspaper can be put directly onto the clay. Fit the wet cloths over the wire and as an added precaution place a moist sponge on the top of the head. Then the airtight material.

For a figure, build a wooden frame that can be slipped on and off. Cover the top and three sides with air-resisting stuff. The fourth side is a flap that can be thumbtacked onto the wooden frame. You now have a fairly airtight compartment similar to the can you first used. Put wet rags and wet newspapers over the figure. Only experience will teach you how much weight the clay will stand and how wet the cloths and newspapers should be; not dripping. After the first day

CONSTRUCTION OF AIRTIGHT COMPARTMENT

Tack your airtight material—oilcloth or rubber sheeting—on the top, back and two sides of a wooden frame like the one here illustrated. The front should be a loose flap of the same material. The flap can be thumbtacked down after the compartment is put in position. This airtight contrivance can be easily removed and replaced.

you will be able to judge whether your precautions have been adequate.

Should the work dry through no fault of your own, do not despair. For it can be softened—with time. *Do not* pour water over the clay. It wets only the surface. It does not penetrate. It runs off. We have given you directions for moistening dry clay on a small design. We give them again. Punch holes all over the clay with a nail. Fill them with water. Cover the figure with the moist rags and papers as before. And wait a day or two for the water to penetrate.

Do not smear clay over cracks in the innocent belief that they are then mended. A crack is not superficial. Should one occur, take a narrow modeling tool and press it into the crack as far as possible. Fill this space with clay. And don't slight the process. When carelessly done, water seeps into the crack and undermines the clay at the point where it adheres to the armature. Then a whole section may break off.

There is nothing mysterious about any of these processes, and nothing creative. We have suggested a few of the technical devices sculptors have adopted and adapted.

Chapter V. MODELING A FIGURE

~~~~~~

THIS chapter on building up a piece of sculpture with an armature will present another technical aspect of modeling. If, during later work, others arise, you will be able to solve them yourself by way of your own experience. Aesthetic aspects depend on individual vision and creative power. You have already found yours greater than you had any idea. Sufficient skill to master craftsmanship is definitely within your scope. Once you have mastered the technical mechanical difficulties, they are mastered forever.

In an effort to simplify your task we have devoted a page to a graphic example of an armature and a detailed description. Give it the benefit of some attentive study. We have made the picture with its description to approximate, as closely as possible, the actual handling of the materials themselves.

We are showing you an example of an armature for a standing figure. After you have built it, you will see how it can be readjusted to meet the form of a sitting figure or one lying down.

Some of the difficulty of presentation lies in the fact that every process interlocks and embodies every other. You cannot build your armature until you are clear about the shapes you are building it to support.

Therefore, we ask you to read the whole chapter through before you start work. We hope this will give you a feel of the entire process, and a sense of the inter-relation of all parts. We shall not be able to say, Now do this; now do that. The process is one of growth and development, every stage maturing as in nature itself. Nature does not finish up our hands after she has completed our heads. Every part progresses along with every other.

You can get your plumber to help you prepare the fixed parts of the armature. Our diagram gives the measurements for a half-size figure. We do not suggest your dealing with any greater size. The armature, as you see, measures longer than the figure itself. For a smaller size reduce proportionately, making every measurement one-third or one-half of the figures given.

For a half-size figure you will need to prepare about 150 pounds of clay. You already know how to prepare the clay. The manner is precisely the same as you used for the small model.

An armature is a wood and metal support for a piece of sculpture in clay. Without this support the clay would collapse, almost as our own flesh would collapse without the support of bone.

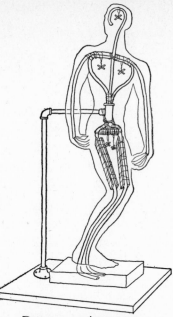

Bolt down a flange toward the back of a board measuring about 24 inches square. Into this flange screw a ½-inch iron pipe, 22 inches long. Screw an ell onto the upper end. Add 9 inches of iron pipe screwed horizontally into the ell. Screw a tee onto the end of the horizontal. (These are the parts your plumber can help you assemble.)

Cut a length of ⅜-inch lead wire. Bend the top into a loop for the head. The measurement of this length varies. But from the top of the loop down to the wooden board measures two inches longer than the finished figure. These two inches allow for clay base. Wire this length of lead onto the tee, upright from the tee.

Cut off about 6 feet of lead. Shape the middle of this length into a torso-like form. Pull the two ends down through the tee. Wire the upper end, the torso part, 1 inch below the pit of the neck. In order to form the pelvis support, spread apart the two lengths hanging below the tee. To hold the spread position, wire a piece of wood between the two leads firmly onto the leads and the tee.

Cut a length of lead measuring the width of the shoulders plus the length of the arms. Wire this to the perpendicular just above the torso lead.

Bend the lead parts of the armature to indicate the action of the figure. Bend the foot ends so that they will rest inside the 2-inch clay base.

Reinforce the thighs with strips of wood wired to the armature.

Place the butterflies where they are needed for support.

Think, then, of an armature as a skeleton. And always think of it in close relation to your design almost as our own skeletons are related to our bodies. The skeleton, the armature, must follow the action of your design.

Once you have built your armature and have started large-scale work it is almost impossible to make major changes. For this reason the galvanized iron pipe (see illustration) is longer than the actual dimensions of the figure. This gives you an opportunity to make a thick base, 2 inches for a 36-inch figure. If it becomes necessary to lengthen the figure, raising the shoulders will be almost impossible without destroying much of the work already accomplished. It is a simple matter to cut down the base and lower the feet. A base thicker than you desire can be corrected in casting.

You don't want the mechanical difficulties involved in altering an armature or in working with an unsuitable one to get in the way of creative work. We stress this because students often build the armature thoughtlessly. It then becomes a hindrance, leading to discouraging difficulties rather than being a help toward avoiding them.

The mechanical job of building an armature can also be a creative process. For you must feel the action of the skeleton quite as clearly as you felt the action of the whole figure when you made your first design. As before, you transmit the sense of movement into another material. Though you have only the simple outline of action in the armature you have rich opportunity to make it expressive.

We might suggest this order of procedure:

We advise you to make a small sketch of your design before starting. And we advise you to build it carefully even though it is only a sketch for a larger and more important work. Always keep in mind the laws of design and the spiral. Design your sketch as faithfully as you did your first work. A sketch should not be a thoughtless job, even though the details are omitted. It is a model suggestive of the bigger forms. This sketch should be used to help you with the armature.

Assume that you have the sketch of the pose you plan to give your model. The armature is ready; the clay is prepared. Your model is due in half an hour.

In order to make your model feel the action you must feel it thoroughly yourself. Certainly you have made your sketch but you want to feel the quality of the action deeply in your own body. So, before posing the model, practice the pose in front of a mirror. Act it completely. Realize in your own body what you are trying to say. Notice where the stress comes.

You know from past experience with sculpture that action in art does not necessarily indicate violence. You know that in art action is defined by balance of form, distribution of weight and a sense of stress. There is action in a sleeping figure. Weight distributed more or less evenly along a broad base transmits a feeling of rest. You will never be able to transmit your emotion to the model unless you have clearly established the weight and shape of it within your own body.

Nothing is more difficult to work from than a lacka-

41

daisical, indifferent model. You are not asking him (or her) to hold a rigid or wooden position. You will ask him to realize fully while he is posing your profound reasons for that particular pose.

You yourself have practiced the pose and know all the variations possible to the expression of the idea. Many different poses will express the same idea. You have made your choice. You have already established the general lines in your sketch. Acting the pose in front of a mirror will help establish the forms in your mind. Think of your design as a combination of what you feel in your body and what you see in the mirror. Whenever, during work, you become discouraged, give the pose life within you by taking it again. Close your eyes and just feel. Then look into the mirror. Examine the form your emotion takes. Think as creators and not as mechanics from the very beginning.

The model has arrived. You are prepared now to pose him intelligently. You can give him the idea and have every right to expect co-operation.

You are ready to work . . .

But we are going to interrupt your start with some general discussion. Please don't be impatient because we feel that such discussion will save you time later, for it will give you a more profound understanding of sculpture. You are dealing with three factors: the medium—clay, a model, and an idea. Your understanding of sculpture will grow as your sense of the inter-relation of these three factors increases.

When modeling a figure from life, fidelity to the

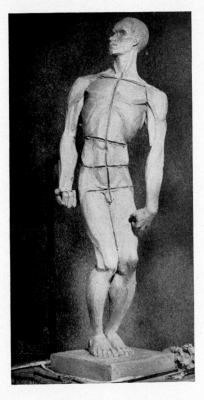 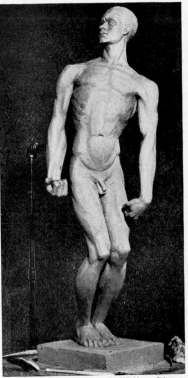

Andrew T. Wolfson Photo.

EARLY STAGES OF FIGURE

The principal masses and the action have been determined. Note the lines indicating the action of the thorax and the pelvis. The two upper parallels frame the thorax, the lower, the pelvis. The perpendicular is the line of action. You can now see that the main action of the torso takes place in the area between these two sets of parallels.

Secondary masses have now been placed in position.

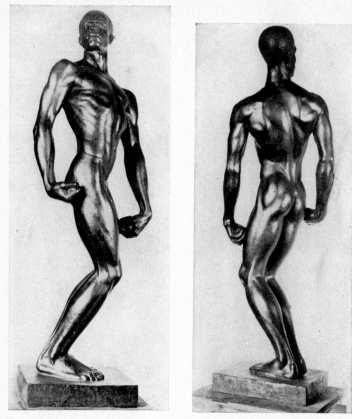

FRONT VIEW OF FINISHED FIGURE—   REAR VIEW OF FINISHED FIGURE—
GIROLAMO PICCOLI   GIROLAMO PICCOLI

model, measure for measure, is a lesser element. It is after all not important if the measurements of the ankle of a leg do not correspond with those of the model. Expression is vitally important. Clear articulation is vitally important—an unmuddled pronouncement of the leg's direction. The distribution of weight is vitally important—what sculptors call thrust and counter-thrust. If the action, the weight, pushes down in one part, this must be balanced and harmonized by a compensating, retaliating weight in another.

It is sometimes advisable to exaggerate slightly movement and size and direction of form in order to capture the emotional, aesthetic content of the conception. You will find as you work that emotion and aesthetics interlock; one embodies the other. As you build up your clay and feel stress and counterstress and the expression of the idea in your own body, examine the model for the direction of forms in relation to one another. You are not copying the outlines of a figure. You are expressing by way of the human figure an emotion in clay. Nothing must be sacrificed, neither the form nor the emotion. Neither will be sacrificed. For, with the interplay of form with idea, one cannot be separated from the other.

Ask yourself these questions as you work: What is the character of the form? Is it wedge shape, cylindrical, rectangular? What is the shape of the transition connecting one form with another? After you have answered these questions in clay, re-examine the original idea in your mind's eye. Then re-examine the clay to be sure that it reveals, not conceals, the idea. Now you will begin to feel the interplay of all the sculptural aspects, technical, emotional, formal.

You cannot approach an alive body as you would an inanimate object. The inanimate, no matter how beautiful, is fixed. In life there is continual movement. Even the sleeper breathes. Every movement is significant, is the result of some basic happening within.

Look at the model for balance. Observe the leg that carries the weight of the body. The upward thrust of the leg raises the pelvis on the side that carries the weight. Notice the compensating thrust of the thorax on the opposite side and the movement of the shoulders. These movements express the main action of the figure. They are therefore the basis of the design. Observe the position of the pit of the neck. With your mind's eye imagine a plumb line dropped from the pit of the neck to where it would fall in relation to the feet. As you do this, place a bit of clay to indicate the pit of the neck and then place the armature for the legs in position.

Now notice the movement of the head. Bend the head length of pipe into position.

Relatively little clay covers the armature at the ankles, arms, and the pit of the neck. The armature at these parts must therefore be most accurately placed. Put the wooden supports and the butterflies into position.

Look at the model and observe the way arms and legs grow from the trunk. They are not isolated appendages or accessories. They are necessary to the development of movement.

44

We repeat again in order to keep you from falling into a common error. Every part should advance with every other part. Then you get the sense of the whole maturing from a central idea and core. As we have already said, if you have put too much time and effort on the last details of one part, you change it reluctantly, even though you know it is faulty.

You extract from the human body the essence of its beauty and pour it into a different material. You are master of this material; a good master, sympathetically conscious of its power and its limitations. As you work you keep your goal in your mind's eye. You have a vision of its plastic and emotional quality. But from time to time technical anatomical problems must be dealt with. You know they are solved in relation to the clay and the idea you have continually in mind.

Nothing leads more directly to artistic doom than a mechanical study of anatomy. A study of anatomy as an end in itself has nothing to do with art. Many believe the Greeks topped all people in their knowledge of the human figure in relation to design material and idea. The Greeks never dissected a body. The more you study the works of the great sculptors the more you realize that sculpture is not based on anatomy alone. Though a little basic information may prove helpful, our words cannot replace your own study, your own alert observation of the figure translating your idea. There are no fixed formulas.

The figure is remarkable for its mechanical logic. You need not study the names of bones and muscles. But you must feel the logical follow-through of the whole formation. This feel will help you follow through the

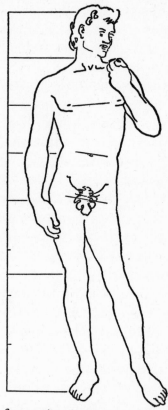

Proportions of figure using the head as a unit of measurement.

logic of your own design—any dynamic design, even one in which the figure as such is not used.

Though the human body is so wonderfully complex, capable of so infinite a range of action, action must agree with the simple, inevitable law of balance, whether the body is in the act of walking the floor or a tight rope. No matter how violent the action, bodily masses inevitably, invariably find their balance. The center of gravity always passes from the pit of the neck to the supporting foot or between the feet when they are supporting the weight equally.

In life an adult figure measures approximately seven and a half heads high. In judging proportions it will be found useful to consider the length of the head as the unit of measurement. Artists often make the figure eight heads tall. If you divide the figure into eight heads the following method of measurement may be used. You will find the length of the head equals the distance from the chin to the nipples. The third length is from the nipples to the umbilicus, the fourth from the umbilicus to the pubic bones, or fork. The pubic bones mark the middle of the length of the figure. From the top of the head to the knee measures five and a half heads. A foot is half the length from floor to knee. These are all approximate measurements. (We know we have given them to you before but believe this is a helpful place to repeat them.)

The torso can be divided into two main shapes. The thorax, or chest, and the pelvis. Most of the movement takes place between these two main shapes.

The spinal column is the connection on which all the large forms of the body hang; a great functional girder on which all the big forms are suspended. It is a great hinge composed of a number of bones partially sepa-

47

rated from one another by a series of semiflexible disks. For purpose of study, this flexible girder can be divided into four sections. They are all connected. Each part has a role, a function to perform.

The first part is the neck, composed of seven bones. This section has considerable flexibility and range of action. Move your neck now. The seventh bone is the most prominent. You can feel it with your hand. It can be clearly seen under the skin. Notice the relation of this bone to the pit of the neck. This protuberance in relation to the pit of the neck places the position of the neck in relation to the shoulders. (You might refer back to the illustration of Queen Nefertiti. It is a beautiful example of neck angle in relation to shoulders.) When viewing the figure from the side the protruding bone is higher than the pit of the neck. Students are likely to slight these relative positions and thus lose a sense of the tremendous mobility of the neck.

The next is the rib section of the spine. The ribs joining the column form a basket. Little movement is possible in this section of the vertebrae. Think of the rib basket as a solid form.

The third length of vertebrae is the lumbar section. It connects the thorax, or the rib basket, to the pelvis. This is the most flexible section of the torso. Here the greatest amount of movement is possible. (Turn in every direction and get a feel of the body's flexibility in this region.)

The fourth section is rigid and together with the pelvic bones makes up the pelvic basin. Notice this last

section, the pelvic section, from the back. Notice with
what great beauty the buttock muscles join the bones
at this point, forming a triangular shape.

In order to help the clay adhere, sponge the armature.
Squeeze the clay firmly around it. Indicate the general
shapes and direction of thorax and pelvis. Model them.
Then, modeling the abdominal muscles, connect the
thorax and pelvis. Do not throw the clay on indiscrimi-
nately. Indicate the shapes and direction of shapes with
the first clay you build on.

Now establish the main forms of legs and arms.

Check for action with your model and your idea.
Take a small tool and draw a line on the surface of
the clay from the pit of the neck through the center
of the thorax. As you draw it keep yourself aware of
movement and direction. With equal care draw a line
through the center of the pelvis. Now draw the action
line connecting these two parts. Draw a line at right
angles to this line for the shoulder action. Draw a line
through the upper part of the pelvis for the pelvic
action. This gives you a pretty accurate sense of the
feel of the whole action.

Check again for balance. Be sure the center of gravity from the pit of the neck falls at the proper place
in relation to the feet.

Work around the figure.

Now for the smaller forms. Wedge shape? Cylindrical? Rectangular? Relate them to one another and
to the spiral. The contributory smaller forms can either
destroy or heighten the emotional quality of the figure.

49

If they, too, flow into the spiral around the central core they will intensify emotional quality.

We haven't talked about muscles. A beginner thinking of sculpture, of form, volume and weight, will only be confused by muscular terms. After you have advanced beyond the first stages some scientific information may be useful. For in time you will know enough about sculpture not to confuse it with anatomy. Now, instead of reading books, observe both the model and your work. The more you look at your work, up from below and down from above, the more exacting you will become and the more critical. And you will not be able to think of smaller things like muscles as additions. Instead, they will become a natural part of the whole movement. You will not be able to think of your design as an arrangement of many flat sides, instead, you will think of an arrangement of volumes. The more often you examine your work from above and below the quicker your knowledge of the figure will develop. Anatomical book learning cannot in any way replace study of the figure.

When you feel in need of some added help study the work of the masters. Even if your local museum does not own originals, it may have a few fine plaster casts on exhibition. You will see with what miraculous knowledge of sculpture the master simplified form, stressing the essentials and using details to help stress essentials.

In an earlier chapter we asked you not to work from photographs. How about casts? We are against it only because copying plaster casts has been much abused in the recent past. Copying has been made a substitute for thinking. It is possible to copy creatively and thoughtfully. If you feel that copying a plaster cast will prove helpful, work with your mind. As you copy keep questioning yourself. Why is this form simplified? Why is that one exaggerated? What are the basic relationships? Analyze. Study the way forms were used with design in mind and were made part of the design. In the work of the masters a small detail is as thoughtfully designed within itself as the whole. This you can learn from studying casts.

Just one more "don't" before closing. Don't neglect extremities—hands and feet. You know very well we are not asking you to give your figure a manicure. We are asking you to make hands and feet big enough. If you must err, err on the larger side. Hands and feet reveal a lot of character and can intensify the character of your work. Make hands and feet large enough to carry the personality of the figure.

Chapter VI. CARVING

~~~~~~

THERE are three methods of carving: direct carving, the method we are suggesting for your consideration and the one we are about to describe; carving with the aid of calipers; carving with the aid of a pointing machine. In the use of the two latter methods, models are reproduced.

Years before the invention of the pointing machine, the caliper method was practiced. It belongs to the time of Michelangelo, to the time when artists did their own work, when none of it was handled by mere artisans. This method has one mechanical advantage over the pointing machine. Work can be enlarged from a small-scale model. It has aesthetic advantage; it is creative in the hands of a master. Measurements are taken with calipers on a small model and increased proportionately on larger calipers. The process demands fair skill to perfect.

Enlarging a clay model is based on a simple mathe-

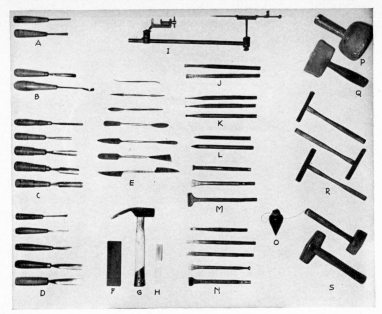

STONE AND WOOD CARVING TOOLS

Collect a few at a time. *Tools A to H inclusive are for wood carving.*

(A) V shaped gouges useful for cutting lines. With this gouge you can draw a line at the far end of an area to be cut. Then as you cut toward this line you will find that it will stop the tool from cutting beyond it.

(B) Curved end gouges. These are used for out of the way places, difficult to reach.

(C) Curved chisels. These are especially useful at the start and for cutting across the grain.

(D) Chisels of various shapes and sizes.

(E) Rasps for finishing, to be used sparingly in order to avoid a mechanical appearance. These rasps can be used on stone.

(F) Oil stone for sharpening wood-working tools.

(G) Adze—similar to a hatchet. If available, it saves time roughing out the large outer forms.

(H) Arkansas stone. This stone comes in various shapes to fit the shape of wood carving tools. Arkansas stones give a finer edge than oil stones and are used for finer grinding.

J through N are stone cutting tools.

(J) Curved shape chisel for stone carving.

(K) Drills for stone.

(L) Points for stone, may be used in roughing out.

(M) Tooth chisels useful during the intermediary stages of stone cutting.

(N) Flat chisels of various sizes.

(P) and (Q) Wooden-headed mallets used for both wood and stone carving. Especially useful for finishing stone.

(R) Bush hammers. These have corrugated ends and are used for "softening" stone. The carver strikes the stone with the hammer to break down the surface. This helps shape the material.

(S) Iron mallets for stone carving. When using iron mallets the end of the chisel you strike must not be tempered—otherwise there will be a rebound.

matical principle. Any point can be arrived at by transcribing arcs from three established positions. When establishing the fixed positions the sculptor usually puts two on the face and one at the rear. The rear point is known as the pull point. This point gives depth; the two on the face merely giving the position of the point on a flat plane. These three points must be accurately transposed on your block of stone or on the enlargement before beginning the pointing process. When you are making an enlargement these three points must be enlarged proportionately. If viewed from the top the points will become three points of a triangle.

Place one end of your calipers on the right-hand point, the other end at the point you wish to establish. Mark this position. From the left-hand point take the same position. With the third calipers, reach this point from the rear. You now have the measurement for the two surface positions and the depth, or pull point.

When finding the points on the block first take your right-hand compass and transcribe an arc. With your left compass transcribe another arc bisecting the first. This gives you the points on the two-dimensional plane. With your third calipers you can tell how much you need to cut into the block to get the depth.

It will be necessary to transcribe the face arcs repeatedly as these change when you cut the stone away.

Copying with the aid of a pointing machine is the work not of an artist but of a skilled artisan. The process is only technical but takes many years to master. The sculptor furnishes the artisan with a completely finished plaster cast identical in size with the work he wishes reproduced. The sculptor usually puts on the finishing touches. He feels responsible for those qualities of texture and color that only an artist knows how to achieve.

Direct carving is done by the sculptor. He takes the most direct and shortest path into the very heart of the material itself. This is a completely creative process. The artist need not serve a long apprenticeship studying mechanical devices. More than any other sculptural method, direct carving illustrates the relation of material to design. The carver learns all there is to know about the inherent nature of his medium. He learns to feel what, with decency, a piece of marble or a cutting of wood can and cannot do. A sense of the limitations and possibilities of material is the beginning of sculptural wisdom.

The pointing machine has lately fallen into disrepute because a skilled artisan could reproduce in stone or wood practically any design whether aesthetically suitable to the material or not. He could copy our very tears in stone, and did. All sorts of crimes in the name of art were committed. Many artists therefore came to the conclusion that only by carving directly into the material could good sculpture be created.

We believe this is not the only way. A sensitive artist with understanding of the creative possibilities of his medium can design in clay for marble or in clay for bronze. But even so, the carver has the supreme satisfaction of working immediately in a final and permanent substance.

For a time the pointing machine did another disservice. Because the mechanics of manipulating it are so specialized the whole craft of carving was plunged into an awesome and mysterious atmosphere. Good people were frightened out of the habit of carving without the mechanical difficulties the machine presented. Why, it is as natural for man to carve as it is for him to create—as it is for a boy to whittle, given a knife and a stick of wood! Some historians maintain that carving is man's earliest plastic expression.

Primitive man created many of our most beautiful examples of carving; and with a tool far cruder than the knife of a Boy Scout. These early works—incredibly early, some of them—are among our most treasured possessions. Sculptors go to them today for inspiration and study.

CARVING IN STONE

Marble is a good stone to carve. Many different varieties of marble are indigenous to many different parts of the States. Perhaps you can pick up a piece where a building is being erected or demolished. Maybe there is a quarry in your neighborhood.

Start with a stone not too ambitiously large.

In selecting, look for flaws. If they are not detected in the very beginning, all your work will be in vain. Wash the stone. Deep, dangerous-looking and undesirable streaks will show up when it is wet. Wetness also reveals color, as your finish and polish will reveal it. Reject any stone stained with oil or grease. Stone is porous and oil penetrates. (Don't get oil on your work, once it is started.)

You have chosen your stone. You like the color. You believe it to be without flaws. Now test for soundness. Take an iron hammer and strike the stone in several places. If defective it will give a dull, flat, hollow instead of a sound ring. You have doubtless struck a tumbler with your nail and listened to the sound ring of the glass. In the same way, listen for the ring of the stone.

The surface cracks running across the face of the stone which show when the stone is wet need only concern you if you believe they interfere with your design.

Set the stone in the workshop. Study it. On which end does it rest best and most comfortably? You remember the paragraph on the natural placing of a stone in the chapter on design?

Now with an iron mallet break off a small piece. Study the direction in which the grain runs. Stone, like wood, has grain. Graining is due to stratification as the stone was being formed. So, when designing for this piece, you have two things to think of: its natural position; its natural grain against which you do not carve. Though, frankly, grain in most stone is not so important a consideration as grain in wood.

In the beginning of this chapter on direct carving we said that you do not copy a model. However, we suggest you make a working sketch. In a way your procedure is in reverse of copying for the proportions of the uncarved stone itself direct the proportions of the sketch. It need not, of course, be identical in size— any convenient size suffices.

Remember Michelangelo's advice. Design your stone in such manner that it can be rolled down a mountain unharmed. Now that you are acquiring a sense of the quality of the material, you also know that holes and deep cavities will destroy something of its essential dignity.

Place your model and your carving at proper working height. With a piece of chalk sketch the design on all sides of the stone, fitting it into the shape. The stone itself will doubtless suggest changes.

Start roughing out. Work all around the stone. Use the "point." Roughing means breaking off the big pieces so as more nearly to approach the shape of the main forms. Hold the chisel *firmly* in the left hand. Strike the end of the chisel with a mallet held in your right. The chisel should all but parallel the stone. You'll soon get onto the proper angle. If you try carving with a chisel held at right angles to the stone, you cannot cut it; you only dull the tool.

Keep your tools sharp. Dull tools increase the difficulty of carving. Dull tools give the stone itself a dull and labored look. So keep sharpening your tools while you work. Keep a piece of bluestone and water on your bench.

Learn to carve in clean, sure planes. A wavy, trembly surface suggests a worker's lack of confidence in his tools and in himself; it suggests an inexperienced carver of indecisive mind. The sense of authority you transmit to your work carries through to the spectator. Perhaps in no other medium is the line of transmission so direct.

The blow of the hammer follows right through the tool and the work. Strike with a loose and hearty action. It will make you feel powerful; it will make you feel on top of the world.

After you have roughed out the stone, start using the tooth chisel in the same wholehearted way, even though you are now in contact with the smaller forms. As the tool follows and creates them you begin to feel the relation they bear to each other.

Maybe in your design there is a deeply cut area. Maybe you now find it difficult to hold your chisel at the proper cutting angle and follow the blow through. No matter how dainty the area or deep and difficult to reach, the chisel is always used in conjunction with the mallet. If a portion of the design interferes with your freedom of action, the fault lies not in the stone but in your inappropriate design. Here is a fundamental example of what we mean by working within the limitations of the material. The medium itself teaches you what is proper and advisable. Don't struggle against it.

When you were designing the model you may not have considered the material sufficiently, though once at work you realize the inappropriateness of deep cavities. However, you feel the need of the kind of dark area a deep cavity creates. This can be achieved by

"BODHISATTVA"—CHINESE—TANG DYNASTY (618-906)—WOOD

Here the free parts are carved separately and joined to the body.
Because of the polychrome surface the sculptor was not obliged
to consider the grain of the wood. If you compare the carving of
the drapery in this figure with that of the limestone "Prophet"
you will feel with each sculptor his feel for the intrinsic nature of
the material.

"PROPHET"—FRENCH—SCHOOL OF CHARTRES—XII CENTURY—
LIMESTONE

All the forms in this figure are contained within the original mass of stone. The problem of design is beautifully solved with respect to the structural quality of stone.

carving one area more or less at right angles with another. Under normal light (light coming from one direction as it does outdoors) the higher section will throw a shadow across the sunken plane.

In carving, give full measure to your forms. Sometimes beginners are likely to make a series of surface reliefs. The drawings on the surface were made merely to indicate placing. Forget them now that you are increasing the volume and plasticity of the design with every stroke.

The work of the great carvers always looks as though some inner mind bursting through the stone had shaped it inevitably. Examine your work for that sense of bursting out from within.

Look down at it from above. Do the shapes flow, are they harmoniously related to each other? If the work is harmonious from this aspect it is likely to be so from every other. Looking down from above reveals the cross section. From this view you see the balance of the forms. You feel the tension. Individual forms will seem to pull away from the mass and yet be held in place because others in proper relation and balance exert a counterforce and pull. And though no form will fly off at a tangent, every one will move and live.

It is important to follow the continuation of a form. One sometimes interrupts another. An arm may lie over a leg, a fold of drapery may fall over an arm. The interrupted form must continue on the same plane. Plastic quality is lost if the eye cannot follow the grade of a plane; the material is robbed of its will and substance. An arm over a leg and a fold over an arm are realistic examples. The same law holds for abstract forms. Interruption adds interest and variety to the design. It is exciting to lose and find the form as the eye travels from one part to another and fascinating to feel the underlying flow in command of the whole design.

Carve all around the block. Keep every part of the work progressing equally. This we emphasize again, and this time we have a double purpose—practical as well as aesthetic. The aesthetics you know. Only by working the entire design as a whole can forms be properly related. But from a practical viewpoint it is impossible to cut much too much away from one area when working all around the whole. If, while carving the block as a whole, you cut a little too much away, it is easy to readjust a few small forms and so correct the mistake.

Perhaps you have chosen a stone that scales in carving. If so, use small chisels, hold the chisel flatter than ever against the surface of the work and cut against the direction in which it scales.

A sculptor who overworks the rasps and files robs the carving of its character. A chiseled finish has more life, for the chisel emphasizes the planes of your design. Overfiling rounds the edges and destroys the clarity.

However, texture, and variety and contrast in texture, adds delightfulness. A polished surface may appose a rough one. Hair against flesh, a series of small folds against a long smooth cloth are obvious, realistic examples of contrast. But do not only approximate realism.

You are working in stone, not hair or flesh or silk. Use texture, then, to solidify the forms, heighten the color, and enliven the surface.

Should you desire a polish in order to bring out the color of the stone or because the design demands a lustrous surface, use abrasives. Thoroughly wet the work beforehand. The ingredients for polishing are water, abrasive stones of various grades, and elbow grease in limitless quantity.

Finish as smoothly as possible with chisels. Then rub with some coarse abrasive like carborundum. Follow with a hone to remove all fine scratches. Break the hone into various wedge shapes and points in order to reach the smaller areas. Finish with whiting. While polishing keep the stone wet.

Don't polish your work unless you have an overwhelming desire to do so and endless time. Time spent is put to better advantage in cutting instead of polishing. Certainly a properly polished stone has considerable luster, but a well-cut stone has life.

A solution of oxalic acid will remove the rust stains that sometimes occur. Wash the stone well after using. A thin coat of wax brings out the color of the marble; too much darkens the stone and attracts dust. For polishing and waxing, use your own good judgment. Neither is a creative process in itself.

CARVING IN WOOD

Plastically speaking, carving wood closely resembles carving stone. Wood also demands that masses be designed in relation to its nature. Though no matter what the medium, in all carving the forms of your design are locked within it. And in all carving, the artist in you liberates these forms.

The difference between carving wood and carving stone is bound by the difference between wood and stone. Wood not only develops more quickly, making us conscious of its growth, but it was alive. With his very tools the artist captures and preserves vitality.

Wood is more obviously and more loosely grained than stone. Graining governs the direction of the forms. An artist never designs across it. The more you work the more you realize that the practical and the aesthetic interlock. For working against the will of your material, the will of the grain, is not only aesthetically unsound but practically foolish; the wood, instead of lending itself to your conception, rebels against it.

And yet, you are the boss. You work with the grain; you are not enslaved by it. Some sculptors, fascinated by chance figurations, alter their designs in the course of carving to take advantage of an especially handsome bit the tool may uncover. It is probably an accidental ornamentation in the wood, a bit of cockeyed graining. Relying on it implicitly will weaken your design; will turn it into decoration rather than creation. Much American wood carving has suffered from sacrificing an idea to superficial decoration.

Study your block of wood beforehand. Using imagination, thrust your design into it. Take advantage of the material and allow for imperfections before starting.

WOOD CARVING—FLEMISH—XV CENTURY—POLY-
CHROME OAK

Though the sculptor disregarded the grain of the
wood he was aware of the growing quality, the liv-
ing quality of wood. Texture is an important element in this composition; smooth areas are made to
contrast elaborately carved areas. Long smooth lines
lead dramatically to the details in the head, stressing
its importance.

"BALLERINA"—CHIAM GROSS—MODERN AMERICAN—WOOD

Here the grain of the wood is used as an integral part of
the design.

Again we suggest making a small model in clay, casting it if necessary. As in carving stone, your finished sculpture will have the same proportions as your block. Before starting, draw the design on all sides.

We do not wish to be dogmatic about making changes as you proceed into the carving, because wood, as you will discover, is unpredictable. It is, or was, after all, alive. Do not be swayed too much by accidental markings and before making changes to take advantage of the grain be certain you are not weakening your conception.

Wood must be well seasoned. Otherwise it will check. Checks are the splits or cracks caused by shrinkage during the process of seasoning, or drying. Shrinkage is due to the difference between the sapwood, the outer section, and the heartwood, the interior of the tree. The larger the block the surer you must be that the wood has been well seasoned. Old master carvers would select their woods years in advance, twenty years in advance. The blocks would be left around the workshop to season.

If the wood comes from large trees you buy it quartersawed—sawed into four longitudinal, pie-shaped sections. Remove the heart. Now shrinkage takes place between the annual rings. This allays checking, lessens the instances but does not guarantee against it. If the wood has been seasoned for a number of years sculptors can at least see where checks have occurred and design accordingly.

Select woods with an even, smooth grain. Any of

the fruit woods are excellent, and walnut and chestnut. Mahogany is beautiful to carve. Until you begin looking you have no notion how many suitable and well-seasoned blocks you can find. An old barn in your neighborhood is falling to pieces. The farmer will probably let you have blocks of wood for the asking. Or the owner of the lumberyard has some well-seasoned blocks too small for him to use.

Oak for many centuries was a favorite. It not only takes a crisp cut, but if left raw (unwaxed) ages handsomely. Sculptors do not carve much oak today because it has been commercially misused and cheapened. It has not yet recovered the good name that bad association destroyed. You may have the privilege of restoring it.

Pine, particularly yellow pine, is a wood to be avoided because the grain is resinous and because the great difference in hardness between the grain and the cell wood causes excessive checking.

All wood darkens and mellows with age.

The carver's tools must be sharp. The carver follows through the blow. He does not chew the wood. Hold the tool at an angle close to the work. Held at right angles, the long thin edge of the tool will break. If the tool sinks into the wood pull it out straight. Don't tease it out with a back-and-forth movement.

Divide your tools into roughing out and finishing. For roughing out they have a less acute angle—for finishing use the longer edge.

Sharpen first on carborundum, then on Arkansas

stone. The Arkansas stone must be used with lard oil. Your drugstore will have it. Ordinary oil destroys the stone's effectiveness. Finish on a leather strop. Lubricate the leather with ash from a bit of cotton string. (Just light the string, blow out the flame and drop the ash on the strop.)

Tools must be constantly sharpened. Sharp tools save time and effort. Dull tools give a jagged, tortured look to the wood and rob the cut of that crispness which contributes so much to the delightfulness of carvings.

If while working you shellac the wood with a thin coat, temporarily sealing it, you can partially prevent checks. To remove large sections from the center of the block, saw-cut it at top and bottom. The sawed section can be split away. This saves a lot of time. Hollows can be drilled to the proper depth with an auger.

Wax (ordinary floor wax) is the most satisfactory finish for wood. Paint on several thin coats until you have acquired the desired luster. Or, you can wax over a thin coat of shellac. Oiling is sometimes satisfactory for hardwoods though there are disadvantages, for oil darkens wood and dust sticks to oil. Use boiled linseed. Allow the wood to absorb as much as possible. Rub off what is excessive. This is important; it prevents stickiness. Let the oil dry for twenty-four to forty-eight hours. Repeat this process until you are satisfied with the surface sheen. Use your own judgment about finishes. Experiment with various kinds.

No matter how carefully you selected it, your wood may check. Checks can be repaired, though not immediately. Wait until the wood has become thoroughly acclimated. Then large checks can be filled with long wedges of the same wood glued into the crack; small checks, with scrapings filed from the block. Pour a little melted carpenter's glue on the bottom of the block. Scrape the wood under the pool of glue with a square chisel. Fill the checks with this paste. The filling will be almost identical in color with the block.

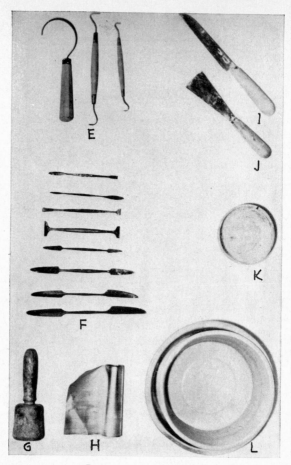

Plaster Casting Tools

You will find these tools useful. Not all are essential. Substitutes can be used.

(E) Steel Gouges. These are used for removing the clay from the mold after it has been opened. These tools are stronger than the wire-end clay modeling tools. However, a *stout* clay modeling tool can be substituted.

(F) Steel spatulas, scrapers and chisels to be used in making changes in the plaster cast if necessary. The steel spatulas are for filling air-holes and nicks in the plaster. However, your wooden spatulas can be substituted.

(G) Wood mallet used in conjunction with a dull chisel or a screw driver for chipping the mold from the cast.

(H) Shim brass for making the separation walls in the mold.

(I) Knife with a 6″ to 8″ blade. Used for cutting away excessive plaster from the mold at the division points. If not available a kitchen knife of similar proportions will serve.

(J) Chisel shaped knife with a cutting edge from 2″ to 3″. This shape tool is sometimes more convenient than the knife. A wide carpenter's chisel can be substituted.

(K) A rubber ball that has been cut in half to serve as a basin for mixing small quantities of plaster. Any convenient size. It can be easily cleaned after the plaster has set by turning it inside out.

(L) Dish pans of various sizes for mixing plaster.

Chapter VII. WASTE MOLDS

~~~~~~

THERE are several ways of casting. The most usual and the best method is the "waste mold" process; *waste* mold because during the process the clay model and the mold are destroyed.

Every sculptor should be familiar with this method of making a plaster cast. It is preferred to other methods because it is most accurate and gives the best impression of the modeled clay. It gives you a permanent record of your work. Clay, unless it is baked (terra cotta), is not durable. A gelatin mold can be made from your cast for quantity production. The bronze caster will require your cast if the work is to be reproduced in bronze. If later you wish to carve the subject in wood or in stone, the cast will serve as a useful suggestion.

MATERIALS

Plaster of Paris (molding plaster)
Laundry bluing

67

Old iron pipe
Shim brass—38-gauge
Tincture of green soap
Salad oil
Burlap—old potato bag
Basin—dishpan holding about 8 quarts of water
Small basin
Sharp knife
Very blunt chisel
Ordinary scissors
Large spoon
Wooden mallet
Camel's-hair brush
Sponge
Bristle brush
Modeling tool

Tincture of Green Soap

If green soap is not available, melt ordinary white soap in boiling water in proportion to one pint to four cubic inches of soap. Add a tablespoon of olive oil. Boil until completely dissolved.

Shim Brass

If shim brass is not available, ordinary thin tin may be substituted. However, tin is not advised as it sometimes rusts and stains the mold. Heavy tin cannot be used.

THE NEGATIVE

We first make the "negative." The negative reproduces our subject in reverse. It is made in sections.

Head by Elena Burbu. All photographs
illustrating the Waste Mold Process are by
Courtesy of WPA Art Project, N. Y. C.

Plaster caster inserting shim brass in the
clay to make the separations for the two
halves of the mold.

The brass wall has been completed and the "blue" plaster is being
prepared.

PLACING THE SHIM BRASS

Before deciding at what points the mold (negative) should be divided into sections, the clay model must be studied with the following requirements in mind.

1. It must be possible to lift each section away from the model.
2. After the mold is opened it must be possible to clean and soap each section.
3. It must be possible to fill the reassembled mold with plaster.

INSERTING THE SHIM BRASS

We have considered the model with these needs in mind and are now ready to insert the brass at those places where the mold is to be divided into sections. A simple piece of sculpture can be divided into two sections. The width of the brass will determine the thickness of the mold. For a small piece of sculpture the brass should be cut into strips about ⅜ inch wide, allowing ⅛ inch for inserting into the clay. For a larger piece of sculpture the brass is proportionately wider. A life-size figure would require an approximate width of 1 inch. Cut the brass strips into lengths that facilitate following the direction of the division line. For those places where the curve is abrupt, cut wedge-shaped pieces. Embed the wedge-shaped pieces at the narrow end allowing the pieces to follow the form. Let them slightly overlap. *Be careful not to form a jagged edge.* (This is important, as you will see later.)

PREPARING THE PLASTER FOR THE NEGATIVE

Oil your basin. Fill your basin half full of water. With laundry bluing give your water a deep-blue color. Take the plaster in your hands and sift it through your fingers over the water, spreading the plaster over the complete area. Feel for impurities and lumps. *They must be removed.* The sifting process must be done both rapidly and carefully. The plaster must enter the water in small amounts and be permitted to sink to the bottom before other plaster is introduced. (If large amounts of plaster are introduced at one time, it will not absorb the water. When you mix it later you will find that lumps have formed.) Continue sifting plaster to a quantity that reaches the surface of the water. Allow the plaster to stand in the water for a minute. Then stir rapidly with a spoon. Be careful that the spoon does not whip air into the plaster. Stir for a minute or two. (The longer you stir the more quickly the plaster will set—harden.)

THROWING THE BLUE PLASTER

Take some plaster in your hand, enough to hold easily, keep the fingers of your hand together and, starting at the top, throw the plaster with an upward stroke. Completely cover the model. Be careful that the plaster enters all the hollows. After having completely covered the clay with a thin coat of plaster, blow into hollows and undercuts to eliminate any air pockets that may have developed, hollows formed by nostrils and

70

The mold has been completed. The iron reinforcements are in place. The worker is now scraping the plaster to expose the edge of the shim brass preparatory to opening the mold.

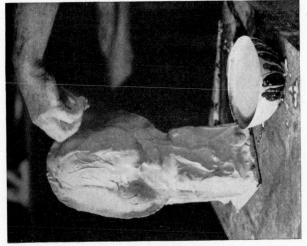

One-quarter inch thick blue plaster is being thrown on the clay.

eyes, for example. Or apply the plaster into small hollows and undercuts with a camel's-hair brush. The brush should be washed immediately. Hardened plaster destroys it. Throw plaster on your model until it is about ¼ inch thick. Leave the surface rough. Let the blue plaster set.

CLEANING THE BASIN

Remove the remaining plaster from the basin. This you will find easy to do, for you have previously oiled the basin. If the plaster has set, do not try to scrape it out with a knife or other sharp instrument. This would damage the basin. Instead, fill it with water and allow it to soak for a few minutes. You will now discover that the set plaster can be easily removed. Throw it away; it cannot be used a second time.

You will probably have mixed too much. This is better than being stuck with insufficient plaster halfway through your work. Plaster is cheap.

THROWING THE WHITE PLASTER

While you are waiting for the blue plaster to set, clean your basin; after the blue plaster is set, mix your second batch of plaster. For the second batch omit the bluing. After you have stirred this plaster, cover the blue mold with a thin coat, applying enough plaster to smooth the rough blue surface. Allow this to set to a butterlike consistency.

Now work quickly. Take the plaster in your hand and cover with an even thickness. Be very careful that the places where you have inserted the brass are strong. Make the plaster at least as thick as the width of the protruding brass. This coat should be smooth. A smooth surface increases the strength.

Our first model is simple. But later, as you become more ambitious, your model may have projections— an outstretched arm, for example. Then it is advisable at this stage to place reinforcements on the outside of the mold. Get your plumber to cut iron pipes the required length. Bend them into shape to conform to the mold. Immerse strips of burlap in your plaster. Place your irons where you have previously determined they are necessary. Attach your irons to your mold with the plaster-soaked burlap strips.

OPENING THE MOLD

Now the plaster has set. With your sharp knife scrape away the plaster wherever you have placed the brass separations, exposing the edges of the brass. (You now see the reason for having embedded the brass in such manner as to ensure as smooth an edge as possible.) If the edges of the brass are not ragged, you will find scraping away the plaster simple. Now with your knife cut V shapes here and there along the division lines. Mark these places with an indelible pencil. (They will serve as a key for assembling the various pieces of the negative.) Now soak the division lines of the plaster mold with water for a few minutes. Use a sponge. Insert a dull chisel along the path of the brass divisions. Do not force the divisions apart; this will break the mold.

The mold has been opened and the clay removed. The inside of the mold is now being coated with soap solution.

The plaster cast is being poured after the mold has been assembled.

The iron reinforcements and the white plaster have been removed exposing the "blue" plaster which is now being chipped away from the face.

WASTE MOLDS

Repeat the soaking of the plaster and the gentle pushing of the pieces apart. You have opened the mold.

PREPARING THE INSIDE SURFACE OF THE NEGATIVE

Remove all the clay. Wash the inside of each section of the mold under running water. Now, using a bristle brush, paint the inside of the mold with green soap. Wash out the soap with a damp sponge. Repeat this process four or five times. When the inside surface of the mold appears fatty and slightly glossy, paint with a thin coat of salad oil.

ASSEMBLING THE SECTIONS

Put the sections of the mold together, running your fingers along the edge to feel that each section is perfectly matched, no edge higher than the other. We beginners have only two sections to consider—one joint. The indelible pencil marks will serve as a guide for putting the right pieces together. Cut strips of burlap. Mix a small amount of plaster. Saturate the burlap with plaster and place the plaster-saturated burlap strips across the divisions. Allow them to set. Now you have a hollow mold that you can handle like a bowl.

THE POSITIVE

Again mix some plaster. Pour it into the mold. Pour gently so as to avoid air pockets. Turn the mold from side to side, allowing the plaster to flow into every nook and cranny. Pour the plaster that has not adhered

73

to the sides of the mold back into the basin. Wait a couple of minutes for the plaster in the mold to set slightly. Then pour plaster back into the mold again. In this manner you will build up successive layers of plaster in the mold. Repeat filling and emptying the mold until the plaster lining, the positive, is about ½ to ¾ inch thick. Our mold is large enough to get our hands into parts of it; not, of course, into small details. Soak strips of burlap in plaster and with your hands place them on the inside of your cast for reinforcement. Now you have made a hollow cast. A hollow cast is both stronger and lighter than a solid cast. Small pieces can be cast solid.

CHIPPING

Allow about half an hour for the cast to set. Now we are ready for chipping. First remove the burlap strips from the outside of the mold. (Remove iron reinforcements if you have used them.) Holding the blunt chisel in your left hand and the mallet in your right, chip the plaster off the mold, turning the mold as you work in order to handle it conveniently. Chip evenly over the entire surface, thinning the mold throughout but leaving parts under projecting details until the last. Chip away until the entire blue coat is exposed. Now you understand the need for a blue coat. It serves as a warning that the cast is near at hand and that care must be exercised. After the blue coat is completely exposed, start chipping the blue plaster, and exposing the plaster cast itself.

74

TO REPAIR INJURIES TO THE CAST

Try to avoid chipping the cast. However, a slight injury need not depress you. It can be readily repaired. Assume that a place here and there requires repairing. Half fill a small basin with water. Sift plaster into the basin halfway up to the surface of the water instead of to the top as we have done before. Wait about five minutes before stirring. Plaster mixed in this manner is known as "killed" plaster. Wet the places that are to be repaired with a soft brush, allowing the cast to absorb as much water as possible. Using a modeling tool, repair injuries with the plaster you have "killed." Passing a wet finger over these parts before the plaster sets will smooth them.

If the plaster is not "killed," the repaired areas become darker in color and so hard that it is difficult to scrape them down if there should be need for working over the cast.

Chapter VIII. PATINE

~~~~~~

PATINE, or patina, meant originally the thin greenish coating formed on copper or bronze after it had been buried in the earth for a long time or exposed to moist atmosphere. You know the greenish look of coins in the numismatic department in your local museum.

Now sculptors use the word to mean treatment of surface.

At one time patine fell into disrepute. When swindlers with the aid of acids imitated on fabricated antiques the patina that naturally formed on antique articles the word became associated with fakes. It has completely recovered from that bad odor.

However, some purists feel that any treatment of the surface misleads the spectator. We accept patine, not because we are less stern or would willingly mislead but because we use it as an added creative element with potentialities in keeping with plastic form. It has been so used before. Polychrome woods of the Renais-

sance are familiar to you. We are not going to suggest
you deal with anything so complex and difficult as a
coat of many colors, for unless applied with profound
knowledge it will vulgarize the conception and swallow
the form.

Until recently the modern sculptor did not do his
own patining. Now the conscientious artist finishes his
cast because no one else can know exactly the surface
quality he has in mind; the quality best suited to the
particular work.

The invention of workable patines grew from the
necessity to present plaster casts in a form that would
do the sculpture no disservice. Plaster is not really a
permanent material. It is an intermediate step between
the clay and the final casting. Plaster will not shrink
or melt or turn to dust, but it breaks easily, soils quickly,
and above all is seldom the material the artist has in
mind for a finished work. Your own museum may have
a room devoted to casts of the antique. Galleries full of
dead and dirty white have alienated many from a warm
delight in sculpture. There was current a notion that
white plaster approximated the color quality of the
original marble. Not only does plaster not approximate
the quality of marble but now it is established that the
original Greek was in full color.

The expense of casting in a permanent material is
sometimes so great that the intermediate plaster may
have to serve until funds can be secured. During this
stage work should still enjoy the advantage of looking
its best.

Spectators who have had little experience with sculpture are unable to make the mental grade from the plaster cast to the cast stone or bronze or whatever the sculptor had in mind for his final work. The experienced can mentally translate from one material to another as the experienced musician can hear without playing them the notes he reads on a printed page.

But even sculptors are distressed by the fact that plaster seems to "absorb" the light and, though scientists tell them this is impossible, for some reason or other, it resists those qualities of depth and brilliance which the artist has labored to achieve; resists the caress and play of light that other materials seem to excite. Patine enables even the experienced eye to visualize more completely the finished work during its transition period.

So, though you may not want to regard the patined plaster cast as the work's final stage, you do not want to feel that the art or craft of patining is merely a substitute or an imitation, or merely a trick way of making a surface look like what it is not—like bronze or brass or aluminum. Wise patining can increase a sculptor's range of expression; it can help him visualize the finished work; it can suggest the various materials in which a finished work can finally be made.

If an imitation of a material is the primary object, then the cast must not have a painted look. The properly finished cast itself can suggest in a creative manner the material duplicated.

Or, a patine can exist for its own sake. There is no

reason why it should be used only to substitute bronze or wood or stone. Maybe you know Rodin's sculpture called "Man Walks." It has been cast in bronze. It has also been presented painted a Persian blue with a smooth polished surface. The color is not only extraordinarily appropriate to the modeling but seems to increase the life of the subject. Once you have seen it in blue plaster you remember it in this stage rather than in the bronze casting.

As you work with patines you will find yourself inventing new ones. And you will find that patine is more than skin deep. It embodies the qualities of sculpture itself. You will see the way certain colors and finishes fit certain subjects, the way one kind of patine can close the door against the idea and the way another can help the idea expand and reach out from an inner core.

Then you will realize that patining is not just the business of painting a surface, but is also a creative process.

Bronze Patine

MATERIALS

Bronze powder
Aniline dye—black, brown, or green
Pigments. Dry color in powdered form:
  Green earth
  Olive green
  Burnt sienna

79

Raw umber

Commercial alcohol—turpentine—japan drier

Floor wax

Brushes—stiff bristle—medium soft—soft

(Size depends on size of sculpture. These materials can be bought inexpensively at an ordinary paint store.)

Saucers for mixing

Flit gun

Powder puff

In the following process a series of tints are applied over a coat of bronze paint. The bronze shines through the tints. The thinner the coats of color the more metallic the finish will appear. The more opaque the color the less bronzish the effect. Though a metallic effect cannot be obtained without the use of metal paints, it is successfully simulated only by means of a series of varicolored thin overpaintings. Then instead of a dull flatness you achieve the vibrating surface characteristic of metal.

PREPARING CAST FOR PATINA

(*Warning*. If the patine is not properly applied it will chip off, peel off, and be too easily scratched.)

First and important. The plaster must be bone dry. The plaster must be free from dust. (Blow off the dust. Don't rub it in.) Mix a little aniline dye with water. Choose your own color. We suggest black, brown, or green. Apply several coats with a soft brush, waiting a few minutes after each coat. Let the dye penetrate to about ⅛ inch. This depth will prevent white plaster from showing through a light scratch or a chip off the surface. Let dry *thoroughly*.

BRONZING

Mix three parts lacquer to one part alcohol in one saucer. As you work, this mixture will have to be thinned with alcohol as it has a tendency to evaporate. Shake some bronze powder into another saucer. Dip brush in powder and then in lac-alcohol mixture. Each brushful of paint should be mixed in this manner. The bronze paint should flow easily, leaving only a thin glaze. Start at back top. Paint round the cast in a spiral. Let each stroke overlap the preceding. Now your cast has the appearance of a freshly painted radiator. Don't faint; just proceed.

TINTING

Mix burnt sienna dry pigment with japan drier. Mix this mixture with turpentine to a milklike consistency. Apply to cast with soft brush. As before, start at top, spiral down, let each brushful overlap the one before. Leave to dry for at least *twelve* hours.

GLAZING

Mix solution of 3 parts lacquer to 1 part alcohol. Again cover surface, using previous method. The glaze permits adding a second tint without dissolving or "picking up" the first.

81

SECOND TINTING

Mix green earth dry pigment with japan drier. Thin with turps to a milklike consistency. Paint again, using the spiral method. Let dry twelve hours. This process can be repeated with further tinting if so desired.

FINAL GLAZE

Mix a solution of 3 parts lacquer to 1 part alcohol. Spray on the solution with a Flit gun. This glaze will prevent the undersurface from coming off during the waxing process.

WAXING

If the cast is small the whole surface can be waxed at one time; if large, waxing must be done in sections because the wax dries too quickly for the dry color, now dusted on, to adhere. Use floor wax in paste form. Apply it with a stiff brush. In the palm of your hand work up the wax to a creamy consistency. When the wax is applied in sections, care should be taken to divide the areas in plausible divisions. Only you can judge what they are. However, waxing half a face at one time and the other half the next would not be plausible.

Dust on olive-green pigment with a powder puff before the wax is hard. Over the green, dust on raw umber dry pigment. When the wax is dry rub the powder lightly into the waxed surface with a powder puff. This gives both a hard surface and a polish.

Terra-cotta Patine

Terra cotta is one of the most successful and convincing of all the patines. Terra cotta means burnt earth. Ordinary building bricks are made of earth or clay, burnt or fired at a certain temperature. If there is a museum in your town it will probably own some Greek Tanagras, small figures in terra cotta. These figurines were once popular household ornaments. They were used in the fourth century B.C. in much the same way as you plan to use your small sculpture.

The color of terra cotta varies from a very light cream to buff and on into deep brick-red and even purple tones. The color depends on the clay used and the degree of heat at which the clay is fired.

Variations of tone and color on a piece of terra cotta are always produced by the baking, or firing. The high areas and the thin areas usually darken because they get greater heating than the thicker and receding parts. This happens when you bake a cake.

Only the sculptor can decide what color will best fit his particular cast. We have made several suggestions.

MATERIALS

Aniline dye—the color you have chosen for your
  patine
Pigments. Dry color in powdered form
  Yellow ocher
  Burnt sienna
Pigments. Oil paint in tubes

Yellow ocher
Burnt sienna
Flat white
Turpentine
(These materials can be bought at a paint store.)
Cheesecloth
Flit gun
Powder puff
Saucers
Talcum powder

The cast must be thoroughly clean and thoroughly dry.

Apply several coats of aniline dye the same color as the patine you have chosen. This process is the same as the one you used for the bronze patine. Let the cast dry thoroughly.

PAINTING

Mix either yellow ocher or burnt sienna oil paint (depending on the color you desire) with flat white oil paint. Thin in a saucer with turpentine to a milky consistency. Strain through cheesecloth. Try the color on a bit of plaster. Allow this to dry. When dry it is lighter. If you are now satisfied with the color, fill the Flit gun and spray on the coat of oil paint. Allow twelve hours for drying.

TONAL VARIATIONS

With your palette knife *thoroughly mix* some dry pigment with some talcum powder. The color of the dry pigment and the amount depend completely on your own choice. Yellow ocher gives a buff color; burnt sienna, a darker brick. The talcum and dry color mixture should be slightly darker than the tone of the underpainting. Try this over your testing bit of plaster before applying.

Rub the powder lightly onto the cast with a powder puff. Avoiding a spotty appearance, rub more powder onto the protruding edges, on the places that would naturally darken on baked clay. It is not necessary to cover the base color completely. Just blend the powder with the base, avoiding both harshness and too great a contrast.

If the cast has a spotty and uneven look, re-cover with the base color and rework when completely dry.

We have given you two patines. From these suggestions you can go on to others. You can invent your own.

INDEX

87

INDEX